I0559100

A HOPE &
A FUTURE

—

40 Weeks of Guided Prayers for Your High School Senior

LEE ANN JAMES

A LETTER FROM THE AUTHOR

As my child's senior year approached, I realized I was feeling dread and sadness for all that was changing. I didn't want to go through that year with such negative emotions. I wanted to do it "well"—with joy and excitement for him and his future! As I prayed about that, the Lord helped me see that I needed to shift my focus. So, I counted how many weeks my child would have in his senior year and then made a list of topics I wanted to pray over him, for him, and for us as his parents. For each week, I wrote a short prayer based on a Bible verse that corresponded to each request. As I talked to a friend about what I was doing, she encouraged me to share it with other parents who might want the prayer prompts for their own senior. The response was much larger than I anticipated and it quickly grew into social media accounts where I posted the prayers each week. At the end of my child's senior year, parents asked me how they could get access to the prayers for their rising seniors...and thus, this book was born! While it is written from the perspective of a parent, maybe you are a grandparent or family member or trusted friend. Whatever your situation, I am praying that you are blessed by this journey and am confident that your senior will benefit from the prayers you will be making on his or her behalf.

You will find that each week has a space for you to journal your thoughts and specific prayers. I am honored that the Lord placed this desire in my heart and met me each week as I prayed for my child. I encourage you to write out your own worries or desires for your child as you meditate on each weekly verse. The joy I felt for my senior can only be attributed to what God did in my heart and how He shifted my focus as I prayed-- from dreading my child's leaving to instead excitedly thanking God for his life and his future. I hope and pray that you can say the same at the end of this journey. Happy Senior Year!

– Lee Ann

"Help me feel that calling as his parent more strongly than the desire to hold him close."

LETTING GO

—

Matthew 19:14—Jesus said, "Leave the little children alone, and don't try to keep them from coming to me, because the kingdom of heaven belongs to such as these."

Lord, help me let go of my child with grace and joy. Thank you for reminding me that I am called to let him go to follow You. I do not want to hinder what Your plan is for his life, so please keep my emotions in check with that perspective. It's so easy to focus on how hard this transition might be and the sorrow I will feel when he leaves our home. Instead, God, keep my eyes on You and the fact that You love him even more than I do. Help me remember this direct command – Do not hinder him in his journey towards You. Help me feel that calling as his parent more strongly than the desire to hold him close. Amen.

NOTES:

DISCERNMENT FOR FUTURE

—

Romans 12:2—Do not be conformed to this world, but be transformed by the renewal of your mind, that by testing you may discern what is the will of God, what is good and acceptable and perfect.

Lord, as my child makes big decisions this year give him discernment to know Your will. Give him a mind that is renewed by You and help him see where You want him to go and what You want him to do. Help him fight against the world's persuasions and protect him from conforming to anything that is not in Your plan for him. Help him not get hung up in the worry of choosing the "perfect" path, but rather resting in the peace that as long as he is putting his mind on You, he will be able to make a choice that is good and acceptable and perfect. Amen.

NOTES:

LET TRUTH TAKE ROOT

—

Colossians 2:6-7—So then, just as you have received Christ Jesus as Lord, continue to walk in him, being rooted and built up in him and established in the faith, just as you were taught, and overflowing with gratitude.

Lord, make my child's roots run deep. Help him remember all he has learned already, and let those roots serve him well when the storms come. As he is faced with big and new things in the next few years, keep his roots strong so that his faith never waivers. Help him withstand challenges and be strong in the Truth he has been taught, so that his faith becomes more of his own and it produces a grateful and thankful heart for all You have done and given him. Protect him from harm, but prevent us from fixing any situation that he needs to walk through in order to look more like You on the other side. Help us remind him at just the right time when he needs encouragement to hold onto his roots and allow his faith to grow. Amen.

NOTES:

STRONG COMMUNITY

—

Proverbs 27:17—Iron sharpens iron, and one person sharpens another.

Lord, please put men and women in my child's life that will sharpen him. As he finishes one stage of life and moves into another, provide community for him that will carry him through each. Give him steady and true friends that will point him to You, will sharpen his weak points, and will encourage him in his strengths. Help him see the value of friends that aren't afraid to speak truth in love, and help him always remember the importance of friends who can help him see what is in his blind spots. Surround him with people who love You and want to be on mission with him. Amen.

NOTES:

FLEE FROM TEMPTATION

—

1 Corinthians 10:13—No temptation has come upon you except what is common to humanity. But God is faithful; he will not allow you to be tempted beyond what you are able, but with the temptation he will also provide the way out so that you may be able to bear it.

Lord, help my child understand that he will be tempted and please remove the stigma of admitting temptation. Help him recognize it and acknowledge it and be willing to voice it. Surround him with friends that do not judge him for these admissions, but rather encourage honesty so that they can all be stronger together. Help them realize that it is common, and that You have already prepared them for it. Remind my child that it is not more than he can bear, if he brings it to You. Remind him that with You, he can endure it. As he moves on to an adult life without our supervision, help him stand strong when the temptations come and help him find the way out that You have already prepared for him. Amen.

NOTES:

ENJOYMENT DURING SENIOR YEAR

—

John 10:10—A thief comes only to steal and kill and destroy. I have come so that they may have life and have it in abundance.

Lord, help my child remember that You desire for him to live a full and abundant life. As his Good Shepherd, you are the opposite of the one who wants to steal, kill, and destroy. You want to give him a sense of security and freedom. Help him not feel bogged down with worries, but rather be able to enjoy the possibilities ahead of him and find enjoyment this year. Help him have a year of abundance that is filled with Your joy and peace. Grant him good memories with friends that will disperse after this year, and give them opportunities to serve each other and You as the leaders of their school. Amen.

NOTES:

HUNGER FOR GOD'S WORD

—

John 6:33-35—"For the bread of God is the one who comes down from heaven and gives life to the world." Then they said, "Sir, give us this bread always." "I am the bread of life," Jesus told them. "No one who comes to me will ever be hungry, and no one who believes in me will ever be thirsty again.

Lord, help my child always hunger for you and your Word. When things feel "off" in his life, help him recognize any area of his life that is starving for You. Remind him that only You can fulfill his greatest needs and inmost desires, and protect him from seeking gratification anywhere else. Keep him hungry for only the things that You desire in his life and make anything else unappetizing to him. I want him to look back on his life and realize that he was never hungry or thirsty because You had already provided. Help him live in such a way that he would be able to do so. Amen.

NOTES:

APPRECIATION FOR THE POWER OF GOD

—

Luke 5:26—Then everyone was astounded, and they were giving glory to God. And they were filled with awe and said, "We have seen incredible things today."

Lord, help my child witness and appreciate the wonder of You. Give him real world experiences that are clearly Your power at work so that he can understand the depth and width of Your power and love. Put him in places that allow him to be amazed at You and what You can do. Help him to recognize the extraordinary as more than coincidence or good luck. Allow him to bear witness to Your power and fill him with awe for Your glory. Amen.

NOTES:

RELATIONSHIP WITH PARENTS

—

Proverbs 1:8-9—Listen, my son, to your father's instruction, and don't reject your mother's teaching, for they will be a garland of favor on your head and pendants around your neck.

Lord, as my child desires and seeks more independence from us during this year, help him remember that our instruction and guidance are meant to help him. Give us wisdom on when to loosen the reins, and soften his heart towards hearing and accepting our teaching so that he will live a life of obedience. Help him see the end game of an obedient life that results in being granted authority and positions of honor according to Your Word. Amen.

NOTES:

Then everyone was astounded, and they were giving glory to God. And they were filled with awe and said, "We have seen incredible things today."

LUKE 5:26

WISDOM

—

Proverbs 2:6—For the Lord gives wisdom; from his mouth come knowledge and understanding.

Lord, as my child matures and pursues his calling, help him understand the difference between knowledge and wisdom. Help him recognize that wisdom comes from You, and through that comes true knowledge and understanding. Protect him from being confused by any thought or lesson that presents itself as education or higher-thinking if that lesson is not in line with Your Truth. Help him seek Your wisdom as his ultimate source of information, and through that source grant him the ability and resources he needs to serve You well in all that he does. Amen.

NOTES:

WEEK 11
SAFETY

—

Psalm 121:8—The Lord will protect your coming and going both now and forever.

Lord, thank you for the promise that You will watch over my child now and forever. As we release him into the world and out from under our protection, please keep him safe. Help him remember all the lessons we have taught him about making wise decisions, and help us rest in the promise of Your love for him. Put a hedge of protection around him and keep him from harm, according to Your will. We ask for health, safety, and Your close eye on him both now and forevermore. Amen.

NOTES:

WEEK 12

FUTURE SPOUSE

—

1 John 4:8—The one who does not love does not know God, because God is love.

Lord, I pray that my child would find someone who loves You more than she loves him and who knows and serves You with her whole heart. After her love for You, help her love him fully and without abandon. Let her be someone that he can have fun with, make a difference with, and as a couple point others to You. I pray she would be someone who appreciates all the wonderful things about him. Please help him always remember to serve her according to Your word. Let him find a love that endures all things and is an example of Your love for us. Amen.

NOTES:

HONOR THE LORD WITH CHOICES

—

Galatians 6:9—Let us not get tired of doing good, for we will reap at the proper time if we don't give up.

Lord, I pray that my child would not grow weary in choosing good over easy. Give him an eternal perspective as he walks through the next few formative years, reminding him that following Your path is always best. Help him be strong and make wise choices, even when he feels alone in those decisions. May his goal always be to honor and point others to You. When times get tough, remind him of the harvest to come if he does not give up. Make him brave enough to stand alone and stay strong if he needs to do so. Remind him that his choices will define him and either make much or little of You. Amen.

NOTES:

BE A LEADER FOR CHRIST

—

James 1:12—Blessed is the one who endures trials, because when he has stood the test he will receive the crown of life that God[a] has promised to those who love him.

Lord, I pray that my child would persevere when the trials come. When he is faced with difficult situations and choices, give him the courage to be a leader for You and withstand the tests he will encounter. Remind him of Your promises for those who love You, and help him lead others in that same way. Place him in positions of leadership where he can point others to You, and remind him to do so when given the opportunity. Help him live and lead in such a way that he will receive the crown of life that You promise. Amen.

NOTES:

THANKFULNESS

—

Luke 12:48—But the one who did not know and did what deserved punishment will receive a light beating. From everyone who has been given much, much will be required; and from the one who has been entrusted with much, even more will be expected.

Lord, help my child realize how much he has been given and continue to grow a thankful heart within him for his talents and abilities. Help him see the opportunities he has received as a blessing from You and prompt him to give his all to them, so that ultimately he can give glory to You through his efforts. Remind him that You have entrusted him with much, and therefore much will be expected. May he always seek to glorify You with what he has, what he does, and how he lives. Amen.

NOTES:

PRIORITIZE TIME CORRECTLY

—

Ephesians 5:15-16—But the news about him spread even more, and large crowds would come together to hear him and to be healed of their sicknesses. Yet he often withdrew to deserted places and prayed.

Lord, as my child goes out into the world on his own help him make the best use of time. Help him act wisely as he prioritizes each day, reminding him to put You first. In those moments where he might be tempted to be lazy or irresponsible, prompt him to use his time and talents for Your glory. When it is time to rest, help him rest. When it is time to work, make him diligent. When it is time for fun, give him joy and a carefree heart so that he can live life to the fullest. Help him walk carefully and intentionally throughout each day. Amen.

NOTES:

FIND FAVOR WITH PROFESSORS

—

Luke 2:52—And Jesus grew in wisdom and stature, with God and with people.

Lord, as my child begins to carve out his path and future, help him find favor with You and those who can help guide him. Provide him with professors that will give godly direction and advice, and help him gain respect from them. Provide him with mentors that will help him grow in wisdom and stature, so that he will remain on the path You desire for him. Let his work always reflect his best efforts and may it earn him admiration from those who will make decisions about his future. Amen.

NOTES:

BE A LIGHT

—

Matthew 5:16—In the same way, let your light shine before others, so that they may see your good works and give glory to your Father in heaven.

Lord, let my child be a light for You. As he makes his mark in this world, let Your love shine through him so that he points others to You. Let his work, attitude, effort, character, and kindness mark him as different so that others recognize and desire to know why. Remind him that his good deeds may be the only version of You that some people may see. Let Your light shine so brightly through him that Your reflection is the only thing that world sees in his presence. Amen.

NOTES:

GAINED PERSPECTIVE

—

Luke 2:40—The boy grew up and became strong, filled with wisdom, and God's grace was on him.

Lord, help my child understand that each year will bring wisdom and a better perspective on life. When things don't make sense or he navigates new adventures, remind him to listen to those who have already gained the perspective that he lacks. Make him teachable and appreciative of wisdom that older believers share with him. Help him discern between what is important and what is not. When he is worrying about something that truly doesn't matter, encourage him to let it go and focus on Your best for him. Amen.

NOTES:

WAY TO GO!

YOU'RE HALFWAY THERE.

—

Congratulations! You have made it half way through this senior year! I anticipate that you are looking forward to a new calendar year when your senior will graduate and move ahead to whatever new journey awaits him. If a little bit of dread has started to creep back in out of nowhere and surprise you, well that's normal! I remember when my child was a toddler thinking that his graduation year sounded like a futuristic number and a lifetime away – and then all of sudden it was here. Through writing this guide, the Lord clearly showed me that joy and happiness can coexist with grief. You can be thrilled for all the exciting adventures that lay ahead for your child, yet simultaneously grieve the loss of the curly-headed little boy who was obsessed with dinosaurs and any kind of ball he could get his hands on. I applaud you for keeping up with this discipline and keeping the dread at bay as you focus on praying for all the things you want for your child as he leaves your home. Wisdom. Favor. Opportunities to serve. Hunger for God's Word. A healthy relationship with you and your family. As you move into the downhill slope, I'm praying that you can enjoy and make the most of the exciting months to come, that you can store away precious moments with your child, and that you can be truly excited and joyful about this new stage of life. May your graduate go and be a warrior for Christ and shine His light brightly in the places God has planned for them!

COMPASSION FOR OTHERS

—

1 Peter 3:8—Finally, all of you be like-minded and sympathetic, love one another, and be compassionate and humble.

Lord, help my child always see others as you do and have compassion for them. Break his heart for what breaks Yours, and let him always be sympathetic to those who are hurting or are in need. Let his first response always be love and humility so that others will always see You in him. When anyone acts towards him in anger or unkind ways, help him see past what is on the surface and recognize any pain or suffering that is the root of their actions so that he can respond as You would. Amen.

NOTES:

OBEDIENCE TO CHRIST

—

Psalm 128:1—How happy is everyone who fears the Lord, who walks in his ways!

Lord, help my child always have a healthy fear of You. Remind him that being within Your boundaries and guidance for him is the safest and most peaceful place to be. When hard choices present themselves, help him be obedient to Your word. Provide him with friends who point him back to scripture, remind him to prayerfully seek Your will, let his greatest desire always be to follow Your prompting, and bless his efforts when he obeys. Amen.

NOTES:

DON'T LIMIT GOD

—

Ephesians 3:20—Now to him who is able to do above and beyond all that we ask or think according to the power that works in us—

Lord, reveal Yourself in such a way that my child is continually amazed at Your power. Help him experience Your greatness and work through him so that he never doubts Your provision. Remind him that You can do more than he can even dream of or ask for, and when he feels like something is impossible, show him that You can do more than he could ever imagine. Convict him when he limits You and forgets what You can do. Let Your power work within him and through him so that others see You when they know him. Amen.

NOTES:

SPIRITUAL GROWTH

—

Hebrews 6:1a—Therefore, let us leave the elementary teaching about Christ and go on to maturity...

Lord, as my child moves on to secondary education, help him also move beyond elementary teachings of You. Move him towards maturity personally and emotionally, but most importantly spiritually. Give him a desire to know You more and to crave Your word and guidance. When this growth occurs, help us to recognize and acknowledge it so that we can encourage him and his obedience. Refine him and let the next few years grow him into the man of God that You want him to be. Amen.

NOTES:

RELATIONSHIP WITH ROOMMATES

—

Proverbs 18:24—One with many friends may be harmed, but there is a friend who stays closer than a brother.

Lord, help my child find friends and roommates that will be reliable and stick closer than a brother. Help him be a reliable, considerate, and kind friend to all the new people he is going to meet. Give him friendships that will last a lifetime and refine him to be more like You. We know that Your word tells us that we are better together than alone, so please provide him with a community of believers that are fun, kind, and strong followers of You. Amen.

NOTES:

MENTORS

—

Hebrews 13:7—Remember your leaders who have spoken God's word to you. As you carefully observe the outcome of their lives, imitate their faith.

Lord, please help my child find mentors who will speak Your word to him. Help him recognize why they are different and the reason for their way of life so that he will want to imitate their faith. Prepare divine interventions for him so that he comes into contact with those who will shape him into the man that You want him to be. Please give them the time and desire to pour into my child and help him make it a priority to always seek wise counsel and model his life after those who have followed You faithfully. Amen.

NOTES:

BRING SIN INTO LIGHT

—

Ephesians 5:8,11—For you were once darkness, but now you are light in the Lord. Walk as children of light—Don't participate in the fruitless works of darkness, but instead expose them.

Lord, whenever my child is tempted to hide sin, I pray that You would expose it quickly. Shine a light on it and don't let it take root. When he has sinned, make him quick to confess. Surround him with believers and friends that he trusts and with whom he can be vulnerable. Make his conviction come quickly and his confession be full and genuine. Let it be received with grace and love and help his reconciliation with You be complete when he brings his sin into the light. Amen.

NOTES:

FIND A CHURCH HOME

—

2 John 1:9—Anyone who does not remain in Christ's teaching but goes beyond it does not have God. The one who remains in that teaching, this one has both the Father and the Son.

Lord, as my child goes out on his own help him always remember the importance of finding a place to worship and learn more about You. Help him find a church that teaches Your truth, and provide him with wisdom and discernment to determine whether You are at work there and whether the teaching is aligned with Your word. If it is not, let the Holy Spirit stir uneasiness in his spirit so that he knows to find somewhere teaching biblical truth and with leaders that are humbly seeking Your guidance. Let him find a church that provides a community of believers that will sharpen him and keep him focused on You. Amen.

NOTES:

SEEK GOD FIRST

—

Matthew 6:33—But seek first the kingdom of God[a] and his righteousness, and all these things will be provided for you.

Lord, help my child seek You above all things. When he starts to feel overwhelmed or worried, remind him that You promise to handle anything that could overwhelm him as long as he seeks You. So many new opportunities and people and experiences await him; help him not be distracted and keep his priorities in line. Prompt him to spend time with You and do things that stir his affections for You so that You are the only true need he has. Create within him an appetite for You that is never filled. Amen.

NOTES:

INCREASE IN FAITH

—

1 Timothy 6:11—But you, man of God, flee from these things, and pursue righteousness, godliness, faith, love, endurance, and gentleness.

Lord, help my child flee from anything that is not of You. Put him in situations that prompt him to pursue righteousness. Give him friends that encourage him to seek after godliness, perseverance, and gentleness. Remind him to act and respond in love and with empathy and humility. And let the challenges that he will face increase his faith in You so that he never questions Your wisdom, Your trustworthiness, or Your plan. Amen.

NOTES:

The boy grew up and became strong, filled with wisdom, and God's grace was on him.

LUKE 2:40

GLORIFY GOD IN ALL

—

1 Peter 4:11—If anyone speaks, let it be as one who speaks God's words; if anyone serves, let it be from the strength God provides, so that God may be glorified through Jesus Christ in everything. To him be the glory and the power forever and ever. Amen.

Lord, help all that my child does be glorifying to You. He is entering a new phase of life where he will be relying more on his own judgment and wisdom rather than ours; remind him of the importance of his words and the source of his strength. Speak through him and let anything that he does be guided by Your direction so that he serves by Your strength alone. Let him live in a way that brings glory to You forever and ever. Amen.

NOTES:

SEE THE WORLD THROUGH GOD'S EYES

—

1 Samuel 16:7b—Humans do not see what the Lord sees, for humans see what is visible, but the Lord sees the heart.

Lord, help my child have Your eyes. As he meets so many new people in the next few years, give him Your vision for them. Let him look beyond the superficial outward appearances. Help him see beyond what they wear, how they talk, and even how they carry themselves so that he can, with Your discernment, know what they need and how to serve them. Show him what You can see in their innermost being so that he can love them like You do. Amen.

NOTES:

INCREASING FAITH

—

Hebrews 10:23—Let us hold on to the confession of our hope without wavering, since he who promised is faithful.

Lord, help my child's hope never waiver. As he goes through new life stages and challenges, may he always remember that You are faithful. Whatever may come, help him draw on his experiences that have shown him Your faithfulness and remind him that You are sure and steady. Let these years deepen and grow his faith in You even more so that he will be ready to lead his family and others to You. Amen.

NOTES:

PROTECTION

—

Psalm 91:14-16—Because he has his heart set on me, I will deliver him; I will protect him because he knows my name. When he calls out to me, I will answer him; I will be with him in trouble. I will rescue him and give him honor. I will satisfy him with a long life and show him my salvation.

Lord, I pray that my child will love and acknowledge You all the days of his life. I know that You don't promise a perfect future for my child, but Your word says that You will protect those who have chosen You. Help my child always follow Your path so that when he calls on You, You will answer. Lord, it's so hard to loosen my control and protection over my child, so I choose to trust Your words that You will be with him when I cannot. I trust that when trouble comes, You will deliver him. I pray that You would honor him and give him a long and satisfying life until the day he meets You face to face. Amen.

NOTES:

SPREAD THE GOSPEL

—

Matthew 28:19-20a—Go, therefore, and make disciples of all nations, baptizing them in the name of the Father and of the Son and of the Holy Spirit, teaching them to observe everything I have commanded you.

Lord, I pray that as my child leaves and begins his own journey that You would remind him of his purpose. Prompt him to share Your love and grace with those who need it. Spark a fire in him to spread Your gospel to those that he meets in this new stage of life. Give him the opportunities and the courage and the wisdom to be a disciple and to make disciples wherever he goes. Don't let him ignore Your prompting when You want him to act and give him the exact right words to speak so that those listening will hear what You want them to hear. Amen.

NOTES:

OPPORTUNITIES TO SERVE

—

Galatians 6:10—Therefore, as we have opportunity, let us work for the good of all, especially for those who belong to the household of faith.

Lord, give my child the time and willingness and opportunity to serve others. Remind him to make this a priority as he learns to manage a new and difficult schedule. We want him to enjoy all the wonderful things that this new life stage has to offer, but help him remember to make it a priority to do good and look for ways to be Your hands and feet. Open his eyes to the ways he can use his gifts and time to bless those in need. Amen.

NOTES:

USE HIS GIFTS

—

1 Peter 4:10—Just as each one has received a gift, use it to serve others, as good stewards of the varied grace of God.

Lord, I pray that my child would be confident in the gifts you have given him and remain faithful in using them for Your glory. Help him use them to serve others and You. Don't ever let him get too busy or too distracted to show Your grace to others through his obedience to You. Help him find meaning in using his gifts so that he finds purpose and lives a life worthy of his calling. Amen.

NOTES:

BE DILIGENT AND HARD WORKING

—

Colossians 3:23—Whatever you do, do it from the heart, as something done for the Lord and not for people...

Lord, I pray that my child would work at everything as if he is doing it for You. Help him be diligent with his time when distractions come easily. Even when he thinks no one is watching, remind him that he is called to act with integrity. Help him know the difference between working for the approval of man and working for You. Give him the wisdom to strike the balance between a work ethic that will burn him out and a work ethic that honors You and the abilities You have given him. Amen.

NOTES:

ACKNOWLEDGING GOD AS AUTHORITY

—

Revelation 4:11—You Lord and God, you are worthy to receive glory and honor and power, because you have created all things, and by your will they exist and were created.

Lord, help my child always remember that all things were created by and for You. Gently and consistently remind him that You alone should be the authority over his life because You alone give him breath. Help him recognize and acknowledge that You are worthy of honor and praise. When the mundane tasks of daily life and a busy schedule start to overtake his eternal perspective, put something or someone in his path that reveal Your glory to him so that he will remember to put You first. Amen.

NOTES:

JOY AS THE PARENT OF A SENIOR

—

1 Thessalonians 5:16-18—Rejoice always, pray constantly, give thanks in everything; for this is God's will for you in Christ Jesus.

Lord, as my child's senior year comes to a close and all the celebrations and ceremonies take place, help me feel only joy for these blessings. Let my tears be based in gratefulness and happiness. In all of it, remind me to give thanks for what You have done in my child's life and what You will continue to do. Help me pray without ceasing for all that my child will experience in the next few formative years. Your will be done in all of it. Amen.

NOTES:

GIVING MY CHILD TO THE LORD

—

1 Samuel 1:27-28a—I prayed for this boy, and since the Lord gave me what I asked him for, I now give the boy to the Lord. For as long as he lives, he is given to the Lord.

Lord, thank you for this journey of prayer for my child. Thank you for focusing my heart each week on protection for my child's future, rather than grief for what is ending. You gave my child to me, and while he has always been Yours, now that he is leaving home, I give him over to You again in a much different sense. I trust that You will hold him close, provide what he needs, allow my relationship with him to adapt and grow, and help him find his people and his purpose. For his whole life, I pray that he will follow You and lead others to do the same. Amen.

NOTES:

I prayed for this boy, and since the Lord gave me
what I asked him for, I now give the boy to the Lord.
For as long as he lives, he is given to the Lord.

1 SAMUEL 1:27-28A

www.ingramcontent.com/pod-product-compliance
Lightning Source LLC
Chambersburg PA
CBHW041154120626
46547CB00020B/3215